Your Wheel of Fortune

Reinvent your finances: Using the power of your income, the wisdom of SAVINGS and the courage to invest.

YOGESH SHARMA

Table of Contents

Preface

My hope for this simple guide is to provide easy to follow and repeatable financial lessons and habits that will improve our financial destiny. Lessons include some wins and also some mistakes to *avoid* along the way. Luckily I became better organised in financial matters when I discovered the powerful concept of FIRE (Financial Independence Retire Early).

REINVENT YOUR FINANCES: Using the Power of Your Income, The Wisdom of Saving and The Courage to Invest

Summary: This short guide on personal finance lessons is to all the younger generation of workers looking to reset their path to financial planning and decision-making. Therefore the target aim could be to achieve financial independence in less time than it took the author to retire from full time work (32 years). However, financial lessons also cover a number of bad decisions that led to failed investments and a permanent fear to ever invest again. But thanks to discovering FIRE (which stands for Financial Independence Retire Early), that fear of investing in the financial markets, and being a part owner in thousands of the biggest and best publicly listed global companies was eradicated using the power of low cost index funds.

It's never too late to recover from failed investments as long as we are willing to reconsider some fundamental requirements for building wealth. In our particular case the two main engines for building wealth and investment income come from low cost index funds and buy to let (rental) properties. The former is purely passive (requiring very little effort) while the latter requires some level of active management. There is no one size fits all for building wealth, but for normal average retail investors (like you and I), it is probably best if they focus their attention on these two simple tried and tested asset investment classes.

But in life you also have to watch out for the risks that will come your way. Indeed there is no choice but to be fully mindful and attentive of all sorts of financial schemes and scams looking to divert your attention and take your money in the process. Adopting a calm and humble 'beta-mindset', our aim as hard working individuals should always be to act like financial guardians taking care of our own best interests and at the same time minimise the overhead of taking on excess financial risk. In fact there is no need for normal average retail investors to adopt any more risk than the broad based market risk (or beta).

But of course the problem is we must also know ourselves because, at times, we can be triggered into operating with an egocentric alpha-mindset. Adopting an 'alpha-mindset' means we take on excess financial risk which, more often than not, lands us into big trouble! For some, it can take a working lifetime of lived-experience (nearly 30 years in my case) to figure out how to become better with planning and executing decisions about money, finance and investment.

Originally written as a set of notes by the author for his (now) grown up children, there may be a benefit to a wider audience of younger workers to know about FIRE and also how to adopt sensible self-governing controls around financial decisions. We must always be alert to operate in a way which manages to either avoid, or at least, minimise taking on excess financial risk (compared to normal beta market risk).

Yogesh Sharma (a Financial Father's notes to his children)

Setting the scene and lessons learned

Some notes for the kids to improve their financial governance…

I had written earlier versions of this guide and thoughts for the benefit of my understanding and then for our sons to explain to them in simple terms our personal finance investment journey. We parents take a long journey to figure out what financial decisions worked and what failed. So the hope now is to pass on some basic lessons from decades of working in different jobs and sectors. I hope readers may also benefit from our personal finance and investing lessons as they seek to craft their own future investment plans.

My 32 years of working made me appreciate the value of time…

I started working in March 1990 (after completing a masters) and finally stepped off the work-treadmill in May 2022 after 32 years of full time work. For me this was a sufficient amount of time to commit to a career in 3 different sectors. But in reality, most people step off the work train when they reach what is commonly referred to as the 'typical retirement age'. This is like a default option for many when the plan is to stop working at the age of 60, 65 or later. For some sadly they may never stop working!

Personal finance podcasts are the best educators on money management because this knowledge is missing in schools and university...

Why did I choose to use the words 'power', 'wisdom' and 'courage' in the sub-title of this guide? I will explain. I had heard this phrase in the context of financial independence in one of the many thousands of personal finance podcasts consumed since 2017.

- The meaning is something to the effect that '**<u>income is power</u>**', which you need before you can even begin to spend and save.

- Then comes the savings part which is saying you need a certain amount of '**<u>wisdom to save</u>**' to create a gap between income and spending.

- Then comes the harder part which is investing, meaning it takes '**<u>courage to invest</u>**'. The act of investing seems simple enough, but it is not always easy making investment decisions for normal average retail investors (like you and I).

Where to start is with a simple framework to govern our financial decision-making...

This power/wisdom/courage, or income/save/invest is a simple framework for thinking about how to gather together our financial senses and awareness. The ultimate goal should be to bring simplicity, consistency and order to our financial house by improving our awareness of basic money moves and improving our self-governance and control over financial decision-making.

The endgame of income/save/invest is to reach a position of economic independence, or financial resilience ...

Of course there may be lots of non-monetary small, medium and major goals you need to conquer along the way, hence this insight into a personal finance journey of ours is based on a process of continuous improvement and consistency over decades and is certainly not something achieved overnight. The process of financial self-improvement is a lifelong journey with life-enhancing effects. *There is no magic pill or potion that helps you get good with money!*

Discovery of financial enlightenment at the late great age of 51! - FIRE (Financial Independence Retire Early)...

In terms of my own journey, despite all the education I received and the exceedingly smart people I was surrounded with in one broad sector (telecoms) working in 3 different verticals (university, consulting and corporate), I still had no positive clear cut clue about personal financial matters. It was not until I reached my early fifties(!) that I could see the roadmap for building wealth and how to invest with confidence, consistency and simplicity. Imagine starting work in 1990 and not figuring out this very important stuff until 2017 ... *I admit it, that's not so good!*

FIRE *will* improve your radar for avoiding schemes and scams...

Before learning about FIRE you find out the hard way that the financial landscape is littered with lots of (not credible true investments but) high priced-high risk financial products and schemes that promise excess market (beta) returns which are doomed to fail. Failure can mean the so-called 'financial schemes' are offered in the market by private entities whose sole purpose is to take your hard earned money, charge you excessive fees, offer you terribly-performing highly risky financial products (dressed up as 1. Savings schemes and 2. Investment funds).

Be on guard for 'get rich' schemes...

Unfortunately some financial schemes can turn out to be outright 'get-rich-quick' scams offered by ruthless snake oil salespeople masquerading a 'financial advisors'. Just look at the cars they are driving! *You have no choice but to be on the look out for these silver-tongued devils!*

Even when there are laws and rules in play, in reality there is no regulation against being conned. I estimate there is a real possibility of anyone losing 5-15% of their *total lifetime earnings* being dissipated into investment schemes/scams (cons) that over-charge you (or simply take your money), compared to just sticking with efficient broad-based mutual funds, or more precisely, low cost index funds. *When you are the owner of thousands of the best and biggest companies in the world, no one can accuse you of having a biased asset allocation (i.e. being too one-sided).* You want to be fully diversified!

Thanks to FIRE knowledge and know how, your radar of senses become tuned into deciphering what is an investment vs. what is a speculation, to what is an 'investment scheme' or worse, a scam (a con to a downright fraud). *The market will never tire of trying to dupe you! Like compound interest, it will work tirelessly forever to take your hard-earned money.*

You must never pay more than 1% in annual investment fund management fees...

You never ever need to pay anyone or any company over 1% per annum for annual fund management and platform fees (often referred to as total annual expense ratios). Even worse is the fact that sometimes some poor old average retail investors (like you and I) can be charged fees as high as 2-3% per annum! Remember these fees are paid for by YOU as the fund manager is slicing off big chunks from the total investment pot – *these are YOUR investment funds as managed and decided by the broker/fund manager that YOU signed up with.*

Your duty of care to yourself is to ensure you pay efficient market fund management fees which are no more than 1%, or even better sub 1% (I estimate we now pay a weighted average range of only 0.25% to 0.50% in annual fund management fees across all our funds which I feel is an excellent win-win ... finally. *Hopefully, you too can get to achieve and experience this.*

You will realise that 'financial advisors' are just salespeople, and some are ruthless...

Remember that these so-called financial advisors are not experts of the money markets. They do not have any deep or sophisticated knowledge about finance. They are simply salespeople working on your 'fear and greed' receptors using slick talk and demonstrating 'voodoo economics'! *Do not get triggered into making hasty decisions and remember that a real and true investment does not come running to you in a cold call, email or social media post.*

Yet 99% of normal average retail investors (like you and I) have absolutely no clue what fees they pay on their investment funds, or how badly they are being exploited, or how poorly their funds have performed compared to the benchmark (the entire market)!

I challenge you to look at all your different investment funds and savings plans, products and schemes and investigate what you are paying in total annual expenses. The most probable answer will be, 'too much'!

Your best remedy to overcome excessive fees is to pay efficient market investment fund management fees...

These days thanks to the 'democratisation of finance' (although I really hate this phrase) you can pay as little as 0.1% to 0.3% in total annual expenses by using great companies like Vanguard. Buying low cost index funds means you keep your investment policy simple and consistent, rather than constantly chasing returns <u>and</u> falling for any 'get rich opportunity' that comes running to you. *This is the difference between adapting to an investor mindset vs. a trading or speculative mindset driven by emotion and compulsions.*

If you truly want to achieve psychic peace, stick to low cost index funds, investment monthly, set it and forget it. For some, they may also prefer to add in a few buy-to-let rental flats to their portfolios since they also like 'bricks and mortar' as an asset investment class. Everything and anything else will turn out could turn out to be a painful scheme, scam, con, distraction, noise and stress. *Just avoid, ignore and move on.*

Just go to Vanguard - one of *the* biggest and best investment fund managers in the world...

Vanguard operates like a non-profit, meaning it operates in the interests of its clients just like a fiduciary, and charges efficient fund management fees based on offering a range of passive index funds (funds that contain thousands of the best publicly listed companies in the world).

The point is, 'managing' index funds can be done with computers and so requires little active management effort by vast teams of highly paid bonus-obsessed financial advisors/experts (who work in e.g. The City of London or Wall Street). Vanguard the company was created by John Bogle back in 1976. John, or 'Jack' as he was referred to, is the founding father of low cost index funds. *He is literally a hero to normal average retail investors (like you and I).*

Alternatively, be warned that your extreme lack of awareness of broad-based passive index funds *will* pose an extra dimension financial danger by attracting you to 'investment products and schemes' that simply amount to massive extra financial risk with no additional benefits in the long run.

In the medium term your funds will tank in value compared to the benchmark (the index), or worse, you could end up losing your entire principal.

This is all because you were steered into buying incorrect financial savings and investment products because our 'fear and greed' receptors triggered us into such high risk get rich schemes and scams.

These will be presented to you variously as insurance-linked savings and investment products, fractional property ownership schemes (such as student pods, care home rooms, hotel rooms, holiday timeshares and off-plan projects). We have experienced this! *As normal average retail investors, it is imperative you avoid taking on any unnecessary extra risk (alpha-mindset) over and above market risk (beta-mindset).*

The normal average retail investor should be perfectly fine and satisfied with the average market / benchmark performance level of risk (referred to as beta). *Experience suggests that alpha behaviour of always expecting super-normal market returns from financial decisions will always land you in big trouble.*

A mid-life crisis decision could lead you to buying a small business which *absolutely* guarantees you have taken on extra market risk...

There is also a massive financial risk in pivoting mid-career to buy a small business such as a gym, hairdresser or restaurant! We have experience of this too. In a small amount of time this decision ends up turning against you with such a deep impact that you realise you could lose everything! The name of the investment game should be (as Warren Buffet puts it) to make more right decisions than wrong decisions! But unsound ill-thought financial decisions could sink you so *please avoid.*

You will find out the hard way that NO ONE cares about your financial situation...

It is imperative that YOU (and only you - because no one else really cares about you) <u>must</u> find your best way to figure out how to manage life's financial landscape which is literally scattered with all kinds of financial products and schemes splattered across social media ready to seduce you, trip you up, rip you up and destroy your personal finance situation which could take you decades to recover from.

It's really a matter of your own mindset and decision choices. Remember that:

- **Hard Decisions Now = Leads to Easy Life Later, but**
- **Easy Decisions Now = Leads to Hard Life Later...**

While this is not something that keeps me up at night anymore, bad financial moves / decisions will literally determine how well you will live in the future...so the earlier you start to make the right plan for you and ensure to keep making the right decisions from a wide spectrum of options, the better off you will be in the long run.

But it is <u>you alone</u> who is responsible to gain the correct sights on and insights into the financial landscape you operate in. Your full awareness, or lack of attention, in this period of time will determine your financial state in the future – so everyone can benefit from a little financial intelligence (or 'fintel').

Financial literacy based on FIRE principles will give you the confidence you need without needing a degree in Finance...

There comes a time in life when you will realise you need to become more financially astute / literate so you can make money moves / decisions with confidence that could end up giving you and your family financial resilience forever. This is the time when you want to make FIRE plans and actions when you are young for the benefit of the older you. *And you won't need a degree in finance to get better with money if you follow the FIRE community approach of buying and holding index funds. You will learn to keep your investment policy simple and consistent because we are just normal average retail investors.*

Then you will thank yourself later in 10-20 or 30 years!...

However, this is only when *you* realise you want to figure out your drive / motivation. No one else cares about your personal finance situation. You are not in other people's plan. You are the same vessel who is born, starts working and one day becomes old and decides to take life a little easier! Hence, it is up to you alone to <u>make *more* correct decisions *now*</u>, so that the '<u>young you is looking out for the old you</u>'. *I hope this personal recount of our thoughts and journey into personal financial wellbeing helps you make the best of your wonderful lives ahead.*

1. Trading time for money, later money for time

We are on a carrousel of time...

When you start working to earn a living, you are young and you have lots of time but very little money. Then later as the money flows in over the multiple decades of working in different roles, you become old and you seemingly have 'lots more' money but less time left.

Use your time wisely to make the best financial decisions...

Remember that we all of us have the same time, we experience it the same way. It's not moving faster or slower for one person vs. another, for the rich or middle or poor. It's the same time but, how we use this valuable non-renewable resource and what big or small financial decisions we make now will compound and aggregate into something either great, or disastrous, later.

I want you to plan for a great outcome. What's your plan? Where do you want to be in 10, 20, 30 years? It begins by writing it down or creating an excel spreadsheet. I developed such a cool financial spreadsheet in 2014 that has served me well to this day.

Time and health are superpowers…

Make no mistake, time is a wonderful superpower if you can manage to 'create' more of it to do what you want to do vs. how otherwise jobs, work and careers end up monopolising most of our time. Health and health management is also a superpower because our state of health condition is not a guaranteed constant. So the bandwidth of time and health and wellbeing becomes more scarce and hence more precious as we age.

We are time traders…

Life's social contract means there is a trade off where, at first, you negotiate trading your time for the money, and later, when you have 'enough' (or have had enough), you can afford to trade your money for 'buying for yourself' free time. Time (to me) is the top super power because it is non-renewable, and having more time to focus on life than simply working has its own set of values and importance which everyone can relate to in their own way. Yet as we age time is also running out as the days, weeks, months, and years fly by.

We are here, broadly speaking, for around 30,000 days!…

This does not seem like a lot of time, but in reality we all experience this same kind of 'life/time travel' where one, then two, then three decades of work seems to 'fly by fast'…and before you know it, we hit late middle-age! Frankly if life expectancy is, say, 80-90, this means 45 is middle age!!! Yet surely this is quite a fit and youthful age to be, and seems far too young to qualify as middle age. Yet we can fool ourselves into describing middle age as when we hit our 50s!

Where did 3 decades go?…

I started working in 1990 and somehow nearly 3.5 decades later I am writing these notes and reflecting on how seemingly fast we 'travelled in time from 1990' to arrive here in 2024! I was searching for the holy grail of financial literacy / resilience / independence all my working life…because the point of finding meaning in 'financial freedom' was to one day realise that I/we could step off life's 'work-treadmill' before we got too old. Somehow I understood in my younger years that time has a superpower kind of value!

By luck, circumstance and environment, a past promise about time-freedom came true…

I recall at a family gathering back in the UK telling my uncles (when I was 24) that I would retire at 40! They all laughed. Okay so add another 16 years and that prophecy of mine did come true in 2022 aged 56. I was way off the original target age/date but my target aim, or ambition, was always true in my mind and I held on to that vision and kept working and working (until I didn't have to).

So thanks to a combination of luck, circumstance, environment, determination to design a future life and bumping into the right people at the right time, it happened! This is because I knew at an early age that financial freedom gives you time-freedom and the ability to do what you want and explore other interests or forms of 'work' whether paid or unpaid.

Now I understand very well that time-freedom is the ultimate form of 'freedom' and superpower next to health, next to longevity and next to maintaining our cognitive skills and continuous learning ability so our minds can take on to new ideas, learnings and adventures. We must keep learning and keep improving to avoid stagnating.

2. Discovering FIRE

FIRE means build 'enough' financial reserves to walk-away…

The concept of 'financial independence' (FI) or 'financial freedom' is not rocket science by any means. Very simply put, if YOU can manage to build up 'enough' financial resources over a 10 to 30 year timespan (that is independent of the home that you regard as your main residence)…it is possible to reach a position of FI.

FI enthusiasts from the FIRE community have similar traits…

Most of the FI authors and podcasters seem to have a common trait of a) pursuing an active to obsessive interest in personal finance matters, b) diving deep into literature of personal finance articles and books, c) then pivoting to starting financial blogs, writing articles and books, to publicising their experiences in podcasts over the internet.

A global community of FIRE practitioners, authors and podcasters have achieved FI in their 30s and 40s! …

There are many fantastic financial education resources available across multiple platforms …certainly too numerous to mention here. I discovered that I really like personal finance because of the positive effect that 'more correct active decisions now' can have in relation to 'out-sized results later'. I only became an FI enthusiast thanks to the FIRE community. Yet I understand how for 99.99% of the population personal finance is a very dull and boring topic. As an enthusiastic money nerd I never get tired of listening to and sharing personal finance stories.

I discovered FIRE in January 2017 quite by chance thanks to Unshakeable…

One of my truly great mentors (a super intellectual and formidable former boss of mine for 13 years) handed me a book he thought I would find interesting…entitled "Unshakeable" by Tony Robbins (a financial playbook for achieving financial independence using the power of passive index fund investment).

Millionaire Teacher I also thank you…

I devoured Unshakeable and then undertook further internet research which led me to another author on FIRE called Andrew Hallam and his book "Millionaire Teacher" (also about the power of low cost index funds for the normal everyday Joe Schmo!). I have been lucky enough to meet Andrew at some of his personal finance talks. I will probably never meet Tony Robbins!

I devoured these two books twice! …

I read these two books twice to ensure I completely understood the key pillars and main vehicle for building wealth (using the power of low cost broad based index funds). Building wealth was something I was keen to do in sub 10 years, mainly because I was already 51(!) and I had no intention of working forever.

It took 5 years of planning and intentionality to get all our ducks in a row and step off of the work-train aged 56…

56 is not that early in age terms but its not that late either. The point of FIRE (just like a recipe book) is it can teach anyone with an average brain and sufficient belief, discipline and intention to take their own leap to independence after working 20-30 years (rather than the default option of 40-50 years!).

The core position of FIRE is 'buy and hold' index funds…

What these two books showed me was a path to financial independence based on buying/investing in low cost broad based investment funds, or 'index funds' as they are commonly referred to. The idea and action is very simple. By buying and holding index funds, you are literally acquiring more and more slices of ownership-stakes in the world's best listed companies each and every month. Then down the road, after a decade to two or three, you end up amassing your own financial 'wheel of fortune', meaning you have created your own private pension or financial freedom fund that is outside of your company pension or state pension plans.

It's the FIRE approach vs. The default option…

The main idea for me was to forge a path that helped avoiding the need to have to work for the usual standard duration of 40 to 50 years! The latter is pretty much the default option for most people. With a plan and intention to act now, you can envision a future step-off point to transition into something else like a passion project or do whatever you want to do (paid or unpaid). So the choice is to either adhere to the default model of working until your 60s and 70s, or you can choose to build up 'enough' of your own additional financial freedom resources that lets you walk-away from the day job in less time vs. the default option. The FIRE model creates an exciting and viable option that (to me) triumphs over the default option.

My commitment to FIRE…

Over the 5 year period from 2017 to 2022 I purchased 25 such kinds of personal finance, financial independence, financial freedom books not to mention listening to hundreds of FIRE-related podcasts. It's not simply about reading but actively working on your life plan to help forge a future path/step-off point to freedom.

Exit strategy planning 3 years before pulling the plug…

It was in mid 2019 (3 years before the end of my 32 year full-time career journey) when I had the clearest ever vision that I would exit on my own terms in 2022. I was going to step off and try something different after reaching a 32 year career milestone in one sector (telecoms) in 3 different verticals (university, consultancy and corporate).

But what is 'enough'?…and how do you calculate it?…

This is why it is important to know what is 'enough' (for you) since this is a critical enabler to deciding when you can make your own move. Hence this is why 'Financial Independence' can take as long as it takes or as short as it takes depending on your specific plan, preferences and your decision-making and action-taking abilities. With the right desire and intentionality, FIRE actually lets you re-engineer a path to financial freedom vs. the default option.

3. Start the FIRE journey, watch the risks and know what an investment is vs. speculation

FI, FIRE, FITE...

Whether its FI or FIRE (I have even heard one commentator in a podcast re-state this as 'FITE' - Financial Independence Transition Early), the idea is you have enough of a freedom fund to transition into something else, or a new line of work and you no longer depend on a full time salary to pay the bills. And thanks to the ton of books, on-line content and podcasts, some FIRE folks have managed to create their very own financial security within the space of only 10 to 20 years.

'FI' was not even a thing when we started working in the 1990s, but now more people are deciding on their own to make their plans to amass a certain level of financial resources from working, saving and investing the gap between income and spend to get to a position of Financial Independence ('FI').

What this means is you have built up your financial resources to such a level (during the accumulation phase) so later what you begin to draw upon it (meaning what small portion of the total funds (like 2-4%) you need to sell in the decumulation phase to live on an annual basis). What you draw upon is enough to support your lifestyle for decades and decades ahead of you and it never runs out. As Paul Merriman of Sound Investing says, you want to be in a position where you run out of life before you run out of money. This is surely a good problem for anyone to have. Spoiler alert, 'you can't take it with you', which is also way the book by Bill Perkins (Die with Zero) is intriguing.

In this context, 'enough' means you are 'rich'…

'Rich' is such a relative and meaningless term unless you give it context. If by rich this means you have enough financial resources to stop working, or take a break or pursue a different employment path, then this level of wealth resource could qualify as meaning rich for you.

Rich does not have to mean private islands, private jets and limos necessarily. Rich in the context of FI means your essentials are covered and you have enough for a roof, food, utilities, transport plus a few luxuries like going out and travelling to local and foreign climes without ever having to 'work for the man'.

This does not mean the default model of working 40-50 years won't make you rich. FIRE enables you to see an alternative, perhaps accelerated, path to getting 'rich enough' in less time if you follow some basic rules and practises and operate yourself and your life with a sense of activity, intention and purpose. If not, you will continue to dance to the tune of others and may do so 'forever' which can be painful as we age. We want to be fit enough to do all the things we want to do when there is an abundance of funds and healthiness to make it happen.

Hence the FI path is an option to buy your time back sooner than otherwise (meaning trading your money/funds for time which is the exact opposite of what we do when we start our careers).

It took us 30 years to, 'get rich slowly'...

It is true (for us) there was no way to get rich quick. So be mindful of that and don't believe the promises made by slick financial advisors or glitzy social media posts. This is why you must undertake your own personal financial education journeys, otherwise financial illiteracy is like driving blind for life! 99.99% will experience the default position of getting 'rich enough' but perhaps very very slowly by having to work for 40 to 50 years. I think 30 years of working (to me) is enough.

You can achieve FI faster than us…

If you have the required amount of intentionality and dedication to the cause, then maybe you can achieve FI in way less time that we did. Maybe you can aim to hit FI in say 15 to 20 years. But you have to want it and you have to actively work on your life plan, job roles and career progression with intention. Otherwise what shall derive is the default option working model where you adopt a more passive and 'hands-off' approach to personal finance matters.

Choose wisely your job and career…

Be as happy and fulfilled in your work for the most part, and you will not be in misery. But whatever you choose, you will pay the price of doing something, or not doing something, because that is life's opportunity cost (the cost of the next most desired alternative choice sacrificed).

The default option is not worth thinking about (to me) because unless you are fulfilled and using all your talents wisely, the job that you pick (or picks you!) could later on erode your mind, body and soul. So job-wise, do choose wisely and do not base your decisions simply/naively on what a certain industry or job rewards you.

Person environment fit means mastery, leadership and autonomy…

So you might as well choose a line of work you find enjoyable, fulfilling and where you get to achieve mastery, leadership and autonomy. Creative problem solving academics call this achieving 'person-environment fit'. But also remember that the race to the very top is very competitive and extremely hard, so thinking in terms of aiming to get to the top 10-20% in a given sector could also be a useful metric to work out how to position your aim in your chosen field.

I had an absolutely great corporate job and worked with some fantastic folks, teams and highly capable senior management leadership. But you can't operate a corporate role for 15 years without carrying such a role. The market place is a real and tough teacher and this explains why some folks stay and some do not. Believe me, the best thing ever is to leave on your own terms rather than be ousted due to cost management or downsizing or automation or external takeover.

Other ways to make money…

And don't forget that making an income can also come from creating a business, writing a book or building content or courses on the internet or selling physical stuff in the digital economy. If these routes gain traction, maybe there is a chance to monetise after some period of practice, success and subsequent experience over time.

These days starting a business and working for yourself in the digital economy is a whole lot different to when we started working in the 1990s. But whatever the endeavour, it still takes serious commitment, time and energy to reach a successful flow of reliable and growing income. Whether you work for yourself or as an employee, there is no easy way out.

Beware the financial landscape is littered risks, schemes and scams…

A note about 'get rich schemes': In most cases these schemes tend to adopt the form of a Ponzi scheme, or multi-level marketing scheme or selling 'Crypto/Day Trading/Life Changing training courses'. There is an abundance of such schemes available out there competing for your attention. In this regard, never fall for such kind of schemes and tricks that will inevitably be presented to you by people in your network, social media, emails, cold calling and the like.

As a normal standard retail investor, your investment policy should be very simple and consistent. You do this by sticking to low cost global index funds (and you can also add a few rental properties to your portfolio if you also like property which we do) because all you are interested in is generating a reliable form of passive income down the road.

Evidence suggests that good solid tried and tested investments in proper asset investment classes don't come running to you…in reality, it is you that go to them once you are ready to commit to such true, tried and tested forms of investment such as properties and mutual funds - which are purchased in your name and which you own fully 100%.

In the case of asset classes like buy to let properties – you are making an active front-end effort and decision to buy a flat that is 100% yours and in your name. No one can steal this asset from you. And the same is true when you decide the time is right to commit to consistent monthly savings / monthly investments into low cost index funds (akin to building your own private pension fund).

But what you have to beware of, and keep a healthy distance from are, slick salespeople and flashy glitzy adverts about off-plan projects and 'investment schemes' and 'life changing opportunities' with promises of excess returns. The risk of being duped is on 100 percent of people 100% of the time that one day they will be conned.

Never think you are so smart that you will never be conned because that's just your ego thinking you will never be conned!

What happens is that a lot of 'opportunities to invest' get presented to you will have layers and elements and features which presents itself as an investment, but which in reality they are just 'investment schemes'. An investment scheme is not an investment, it's a scheme! Some such schemes could be really nasty and toxic wealth destroying scams, dishonest schemes or downright frauds!

Watch out for this. Keep away from slick snake oil salesmen and avoid cold calls and don't be fooled by glossy slick marketing materials about projects x, y or z promising guaranteed returns! You won't know you're going to get screwed until you get screwed! And if you are 100% confident you will never be conned, you had better check yourself as this kind of hubris in itself is a massive red flag.

Watch your level of ego and confidence because this is what creates the risk you never factored that ends up knocking you harder than Rocky Balboa!

I would definitely say with some experience to KEEP AWAY from schemes (actually scams) such as fractional ownership schemes related to a block of flats, or a block of student housing pods, or hotel-room or care-home 'investment schemes' (I mean scams! because that's what they are). In legal terms these are referred to as UCISs or Unqualified Collective Investment Schemes. Please look it up and avoid at all cost.

I would also say stay clear away from day-trading which if you like the thrill of gambling so much, then go to Las Vegas with a bit of fun money - because you know what will happen - the house always wins!

All of these lame schemes are not investments. Vegas on the other hand is surely just for fun and definitely not part of building a pension plan.

You must know the meaning of an <u>Investment</u> is…

An investment is a financial instrument that produces a dividend or coupon rate (meaning an income). I discovered this definition in Professor Ben Graham's excellent book "The Intelligent Investor" published all the way back in 1949!

An investor is a long term player and not a short term day-trader. An investor wants steady reliable returns year in year out and is okay with the global stock market benchmark rate of returns. The most reliable investments are the ones you buy and own fully in your name and which tend to be limited to a few simple asset classes and should be good enough for the vast majority of ordinary retail investors (like you and I). These include mutual funds and preferably low cost index funds such as those offered by the firm Vanguard (and/or a few buy to let flats). Anything else that is offered to you is probably a scheme, a speculation or an outright scam. *You don't need to take on this extra level of market risk because you and I are just normal average retail investors.*

What kind of work will you choose?

The legitimate, honest and best way to make money and grow wealth is based on hard work, application, growing your knowledge, skill, talents, and ultimately growing your value addition or impact on others – which will reflect how much value you can attract in the open and competitive job market. Otherwise the other way is the way Jeremy Irons explained in that great movie Margin Call: "There are three ways to make a living in this (investment banking) business: be first, be smarter, or cheat."

As you do work with a good code, you work hard, your serve, make an impact and keep growing your income, you can also be mindful of creating a gap between your income and your spending. This is because the next step will be to figure out a wise investment vehicle for the gap between your income and spending and hopefully you are in for a brighter, free-er future with less money worries and no debt (compared to our experience).

Here's a small general guide which I heard from somewhere. I can't recall where but it resonated well from the point of view of *you* as a worker operating with a good code. But you also need to think about how suppliers and slick sales people will treat you as all our behaviours tend to be tied up to incentives in terms of how and what we get paid!:

In your career, if you:

***Tell the truth to someone who needs to hear the truth – you will make a honest living** (e.g. a engineer, lawyer, doctor, some kind of* *professional analyst, retail service provider and any professional who truly acts in the best interests of their employer/shareholders, patients, clients and customers)*

Tell a lie to someone who needs to hear the truth – you will make a killing by deceiving people *(e.g. 'financial advisors are just salespeople with minimum knowledge of the money markets whose aim is to get you to park your money with them so they can collect out-sized annual fund management fees)*

Tell the truth to someone who <u>still</u> needs to hear a lie – sadly you will make nothing!

And before you know it, school and university are over and then the world of work awaits. I wish and hope you find something you love to do and then play it well, do the very best at it and the rest will flow including fulfilment, purpose and happiness. Along the way you'll meet lots of people and make lots of friends, but remember that every person in your network will be for a reason, a season or a lifetime. Just don't go making loose bets on people but also remember no one is an island. Connections are important and you won't realise how important until you don't have any!

In terms of fulfilling your roles, and you will have many over the next 20 to 40 years, there is absolutely no point doing a job that grinds you down mentally and physically...*no point in that!*

Remember to ignore the scammers and schemers on the internet who will contact you offering get rich quick schemes with exaggerated returns. Just remind yourself there is no magic here, no one has the 'secret sauce' to making excess-market returns. It took a lot of hard work in many jobs and markets and geographies for us to be where we are today. You will no doubt be in your own adventures in the future.

Also remember that, since our times, the world has changed so much in 30 years since I started working…the business school professors call it living in a 'VUCA' world - volatile, uncertain, complex and ambiguous. Hence you are in for a non-linear life journey from A to B where, as the song goes, 'there's not turning back, even while you sleep'!

ENJOY THE JOURNEY BUT IT WON'T BE A STRAIGHT LINE MOVEMENT FROM A TO B EITHER!

Nevertheless, you will hopefully make 'more' right financial decisions and 'less' wrong financial decisions compared to our journey.

4. Every financial intelligence ('fintel') Step you Take Requires this

Financial Independence (FI) is not really all that different to the classical old school way we worked and saved in the past. People have traditionally worked for a 40 to 50 year stretch, retired sometime in their 60s or 70s and then lived off their pension for the next decade or two without needing to work. So even though this is still reaching a position of FI, it just takes longer because it is the default model we are accustomed to. With a 'FIRE movement' unleashed (Financial Independence Retire Early) if you follow a certain playbook of plans and actions, then most anyone with a average brain can build enough wealth to stop work in their 30s, 40s or 50s once they acquire 'enough' funds and passive income. This is thus accelerating the path to FI (compared to the old school model). But in order to do this you must learn to apply a few essential elements into action as you optimise your financial behaviours and actions required to achieving FI.

So if the big picture is to earn, save and invest, what do the little details look like and where do we start?

Set up an emergency fund…

Well, there's lots of tactics and strategies that we can apply starting with setting up an emergency fund. This was a fundamental starting point for me because as I was approaching my exit from work 3 to 5 years before I pulled the plug, resigned and then retired in May 2022. To be prepared, I started by building an emergency fund in order to ensure that should anything bad happen at work (cost cutting, downsizing or layoff or redundancy), we would have sufficient financial runway of funds to manage all our cost outflows such as rent, school fees, utilities, cars, food and going out for at least 3 years so that our kids finished their secondary school with at minimum A-Levels (or GCSEs).

The great thing about an emergency fund is you will never know what the emergency is until it happens. That is why it is so handy to be able to deploy the cash to fix the car, replace the tyres, fix the boiler. Whatever the emergency, you've got it covered. You are acting like your own insurer, and this is exhibiting some level of financial resilience where you can take some unexpected shocks and bumps head-on without flinching!

But I took the extraordinary step in 2019 to ensure there was 3 years of funding to survive until 2022 in case of a job-related risk. *Most FIRE folks speak in terms of 3 to 6 or 9 months of emergency funds. But you can do what you like based on what you feel comfortable with.*

Clear credit card debt…

I guess the next thing is to see how we can go about clearing our credit card debt. We always operated a habit of paying off our credit cards in full at the end of each month. But that's not the case for most people because at the very other end of the spectrum you might have some folks who simply pay their minimum balance amount each month. The worst situation is to miss a few monthly payments because the debt just accumulates with high interest rates. I have seen ads for fancy credit cards with APRs of 70, 80 percent and one that shall remain nameless at 110%! *Make a big purchase, miss a few months and we are talking financial risk of ruin.*

Automate bill payments…

The best thing to do is to be as organised as possible when it comes to managing your cash flow and managing your payments to suppliers. Pretty much all of us have bank accounts so the best thing to do is set up automatic instructions to pay for things like utilities telephone bills etc. Automation of bill payments means efficiency and frees up your time and head space. *Automating your life's finances is a form of financial governance.*

Start regular savings…

Starting with the power of income, the earlier you start to save the better. Remember this is regular savings on a monthly basis and this is *after* you have already set up an emergency fund. Once you are in a steady state of regular savings this can be 'spent' on buying investments, which leads to the next step – because buying investments creates a future runway of passive income.

Set up an investment account and invest monthly...

Since the name of the game is to invest the gap between income and spending, this means you really have to keep a tight watch on your cash outflows meaning, having a budget. This means you're tracking and monitoring your income, but also all of your spending and I mean everything. So this will be big stuff such as housing and car payments, and the rest like utilities, phone, TV, internet, groceries, eating out, insurance, fees, managing cars, parking fines and holidays!

It's only when you track your spending and costs that you can assess what is the gap between your income and spending in your household, and then make a commitment to setting up regular monthly payments into an investment account with confidence.

That's why they call it PAY YOURSELF FIRST, you are setting aside funds for investments today on a regular basis in order to pay your older self later!

Buy cars for cash...

Okay, one way to minimise monthly payments is to buy second hand cars and buy them for cash. The problem is we get seduced by car company adverts and these days the handy digital apps show you how easy it is to click on your desired car and then within 24 hours it's delivered right to your doorstep. *Convenience costs!*

But such impulses put you on the hook for monthly payments which in time you will come to regret. All of the 15(!) cars that we registered in our names from the late 1980s to the 90s right up to today we never leased, we always paid cash. The famous Dave Ramsey (who created the 7 Baby Steps to financial peace) explains that you should never be spending more than one percent of your net wealth on a car, and if you can't afford to buy a car outright in cash, that means you can't afford it!

The problem is we get very emotional with cars and want the best car which is probably going to be too big or too flash and certainly too expensive for what we can afford because it will come with huge monthly car payments the size of a property mortgage (maybe even bigger than the average mortgage payment). And this is precisely how we end up denying our future wealth growth path because we are 'working for things' when we really want the money to 'work for us'.

Make your spare money work like a dog!…

I would much rather all spare money works for us because money never complains, never sleeps, works 24-7 and never takes a sick day. At some point in the future you will either want to stop working, or will no longer desire it. But the worst case outcome is you may be forced to continue the grind because we are slaves to highly-depreciating assets/possessions because they are tied with financial obligations in the form of outstanding payments. *Working extra years to pay for things you don't need or a house that's too big is such a folly.*

Keep total housing costs efficient...

According to Ramit Sethi (of "I Will Teach You To Be Rich" fame), it is imperative, whether you rent or whether you buy a house that the total housing costs be 30% or less of your total household income. I enjoyed watching his show on Netflix recently where he interviews lots of couples about their financial situations and this was an important takeaway that if you're paying housing costs way above 30%, and perhaps 40% or 50% to 60%, then this is a huge impediment to your lifestyle.

The more efficient your housing costs means there's more money left over for basic requirements like food, but also extras. You can splurge and go out to eat and not have to worry about over-budgeting because you know you have the money for the things in life you really value like frequenting five star restaurants. *That is what I understand by Ramit Sethi stating that 'you can design your very own rich life'.*

All of the above are all part of life's puzzles that you have to solve...

In truth you don't need a massive brain to start making outsized returns for your small to medium to big financial decisions and continuous/intentional actions. Bit it's not a one-step thing - this is a life enhancing process which once all the spokes are in place, the wheel of fortune continues revolving and growing and working for you.

5. Know theses simple financial measures to track your progress…

In FI or FIRE, the meaning of net worth, the 4% rule or 25x annual expenses…Impress the Joneses…

The Hollywood film The Joneses was excellent and really scary at the same time. It reminded me of aspects of our former life in the UK before a new adventure was offered in the UAE. So many people work hard, build amazing careers, acquire lots of assets (a house, 2 cars, furniture and designer clothes etc. to impress people they don't know, yet have zero clue about how much they are worth in terms of <u>their financial net worth</u>.

Households with an addiction to spending tend to have an outward view of what wealth is in terms of what you see (house, cars, designer wear etc.), whereas the quieter neighbours end up being the 'millionaire next door'!

Net worth is important to know because it gives an indication of future passive cash flow income. These days younger people mistakenly think the answer is <u>just</u> cash flow with no tangible assets powering them. No, you need to own assets in order to derive (from them) a future form of passive income.

What is 'net worth'?...

Simply put, net worth is the value of all your assets minus any and all kinds of debt (e.g. mortgage, credit cards and student loans). In other words, it is another way of saying count up all of the value of all the different assets you own such as a house and cars and stuff in the house plus also any financial products like company shares and mutual funds, pensions plans, savings plans, and cash in the bank. Then subtract from this gross asset value figure all the debts that you have e.g. mortgage and credit cards any other personal loans.

How can you know anything if you do not track, monitor and measure it?...

You cannot measure or improve something unless you monitor it. This means you need to keep a track of your financial activities over time, including accumulation of assets and accumulation of debts, income and spend, but the most important thing to understand is, where are you in terms of net asset value?

The 4% rule or 'safe withdrawal rate'...

So to keep the example simple, let's say you reach a point in time where you have accumulated e.g. $1 million in investable assets. The next thing to understand is something called a safe withdrawal rate. This is also often referred to as the '4% rule' and much touted around in the FIRE community.

So this is very simple to understand because all it means is you multiply the 4% by the $1 million in investable assets which equals $40,000. So this $40,000 is the amount of cash that could be generated from this investment fund each and every year. That is the point of building up an investment fund so that it provides you with 'enough' each year to run your life forever! And if you can manage to live on lower withdrawal rates (e.g. 3% or 2%) even better.

Reverse engineer the fund you need using 25x annual expenses…

Another way to look at this to work out what is your total annual expenditure that you need to live on in your home country or where you choose to retire. Let's say this figure is the same $40,000. So what you do then is simply multiply the $40,000 expenses figure by 25, and this equals the implied total fund value of investments you need to build ($1 million) in order to live off forever.

Hence, '25 x expenses' is a bottom-up way of working out how much wealth you need apart from your main house in order to generate a certain amount of cash flow for living without working.

So in summary, remember the 4% rule and the meaning of 25x expenses. It's a quick heuristic for figuring out the size of your own financial freedom fund in your future:

-4% rule

-25x expenses

What does 'rule of 72' mean?...

I like this well-known heuristic, called the 'rule of 72'. This is a great shortcut to understanding how many years it would take to, for example, double your money. In other words, if there is an investment producing returns of about 7% per annum. In that case this investment will double in 10 years.

What you do is you divide 72 by 7 which broadly equals 10, as in 10 years.

= 72 / 7.2% = 10 = the number of years you double your money

If an investment is returning, only 3-4% per annum, in this case it would take about 20 years for the money (original principal) to double.

= 72 / 3.6% = 20 = the number of years you double your money

So, in summary, remember the rule of 72 as a quick shorthand way of understanding of the relationship between rate of return on an investment and how long it would take for that investment to double: rule of 72

Meaning of GRIT...

Okay, this isn't really a proper formula, but I came across it in a book called GRIT. It's an excellent book and talks about how some people have GRIT and others don't. Having GRIT somehow leads to out sized success in life irrespective of someone's basic or modest upbringing or environment circumstance. Somehow they end up overcoming all the odds stacked against them and achieve a sort of great meteoric success in life.

Anyway, there is a part in the book, which talks about how **effort leads to skills, and skills leads to results**. I found this quite fascinating because it went on to define the meaning of effort in relation to developing a skill or skills. Once you have developed the skills, this ought to produce results.

If you want to master something 'they say' you need to spend 10,000 hours doing it. So effort produces skills which produce results.

The question is, what if you don't have the skills in the first place? How is one supposed to acquire the skills? So the simple answer is, if you need to acquire a certain set of skills, then it will require some brand new effort and continuous repetitive effort to literally develop and grow a new skill or set of skills. And by the way, it's definitely not necessarily true that you need 10,000 hours to achieve some level of mastery!

Before age 51, I had not heard of FI or FIRE or read any of the FIRE community books or listened to any personal finance podcasts (the kind which had an emphasis, or bias, towards attaining financial independence). This means I was lacking in FIRE related knowledge and know how (and just owning property does not make you worldly wise enough that you have all the answers you need).

Since discovering FIRE in January 2017, I must be a thousand plus hours into the material by now (books and podcasts) and so what this proves is that a missing skill can be acquired with enough interest, enthusiasm and determination to learn something new.

Anyway, I like the very simple and illuminating formulaic model of ultimately how, if you want results, you may have to get a little 'gritty':

- ⇨ GRIT= Effort that leads to > greater skills that leads to > greater results!
- ⇨ This is surely the formula of a life well pursued/lived/done.

6. Behaviour in life is alpha or beta – money is also lost and made this way

Beta is good but Alpha lands you in big trouble…

So you may have come across the terms alpha and beta. I think for all folks it is very important to know the distinction between these two labels because in life and in terms of behaviours you will come across all sorts of people who are quite alpha and ego-centric oriented compared to others who are more mindful and humility oriented with their egos in check.

Beta means you will probably never lose money…

To be a good enough investor you have to know yourself. I've done all the silly things like listening to rumours in a pub or listening to a mate who works in The City, then buying stocks and losing money! Never act on any kind of financial share buying tips from your mates or chatter you catch in a pub or read in the stock picking pamphlets because a) a little knowledge is indeed a dangerous thing and b) you get caught up in FOMO (fear of missing out) and

c) you will regret it and d) Warren Buffet says, rule no 1 is 'never lose money' and rule no 2 is 'refer back to rule no 1'.

There is no magic potion or secret sauce in financial magazines or talking heads (opinion formers) on the TV channels…

I used to subscribe to financial magazines in the 1990s, and every month they would go on about the 'top 10' latest mutual funds or 'top 10 tech stocks' to buy. As if each month there was some new secret way of making 'extra' financial returns. In reality these magazines are adverts for the hundreds and thousands of actively managed mutual fund management companies looking desperately to attract new money, your money! And what do we do as sheeple? We get seduced into moving money around, making short-term moves which always produce disappointing results. We end up 'over trading' switching funds and buying and selling in a given investment time horizon and all our super-normal bubbly returns fizzle away. *Stop chasing tips and returns as soon enough you will experience what's called reversion to the mean.*

Lost some in the 2000 tech bubble that burst…

I remember the tech bubble of the early 2000s, this is also where I ended up buying a bunch of tech funds and unfortunately I think they dropped something like 30% and had I not exited when I did the value of the funds would have dropped more. And that's yet another problem. We end up like sheeple entering / going into the markets when stock prices are already rising but exiting the markets in a panic when the stock prices fall.

Sheeples buy shares at a higher price and also panic sell when prices crash/market adjusts…

These are terrible investor behaviour traits when what we should be doing is just mechanically buy investment funds (index funds) every month whether the unit prices are rising or falling (this is consistency aligning to a simple investment policy). Falling unit prices (a market correction or a bear market or full blown crash) means you are getting a discount on the unit price which you should celebrate in your youthful accumulation phase of life. The longer you keep investing, the more units of shares in real companies you accumulate and own.

If you want to be a good enough investor, who isn't at the mercy of tips in financial magazines or talking heads on the TV business news channels by commentators (opinion formers) pretending they know what's going happen in the future, the best thing to do is to take a step back and ignore such 'noise'.

Alpha drivers are killers but beta drivers get you from A to B alive…

To put this into driving parlance, you don't want to drive around like a crazed idiot always speeding and making dangerous moves and running red lights and devaluing / destroying your valuable car asset in the process, especially if you crash the car! Since there are ex-ante road rules and regulations at play, you want to buy a safe car and drive in a safe and compliant way always being calm and not over reacting to others on the road.

Learn to yield, be calm and Zen-like. This is the kind of calm beta mindset which will serve you as a driver but also as an investor in the global stock markets. However, idiotic alpha investor behaviour in the stock markets results in over trading, always second guessing the markets. High alpha traits such as stock picking, as and with most actively managed funds, this tends to result in a losing strategy over the long term (10-20 years) vs. sticking with broad based index funds.

Keep your investment policy simple...

So, for the average retail investor (like you and I), the only one single asset class they need to focus on is low cost broad-based index funds and that's it. You keep your investment policy simple and act on it consistently by staying the course. You are not timing the market because you automate your investment purchases every month! As a normal average retail investor we have no access to special insights or knowledge about the future. No one knows the future unless the system is rigged or someone is using inside information which is illegal! Stick to one (or two) asset investment classes (including property if you like that too).

Go for global index funds...

As normal average retail investors, we are nothing special or favoured and so we might as well adopt a 'beta mindset' by buying the whole index (like S&P500, or VTSAX the US total stock market index, or a Global Equity Index Fund like VWRA etc). This is better for the average retail investor than stock picking or trying to figure out which of the tens of thousands of actively managed funds offered by hundreds of brokers or fund managers, not to mention knowing which geographical region to invest in (BRIC? USA? EU? Emerging Markets?!).

Keep it simple and stay the course…

Keeping it simple means all you need to do is buy one or two low cost index funds into which you contribute monthly and this is how you accumulate wealth over time, you set it and forget it. You don't worry about the news and you don't pay attention to the talking heads on the TV or chatter in the pub. You stick to your plan, stay the course and you can live your life in financial peace and avoid any extra stress of worrying about your financial future. Otherwise the counterfactual is you will be part of a very big club of people who constantly worry about money.

Financial resilience makes you feel good…

Once you can get your financial house in order and once all the parts of your investment policy are moving in the right direction, then you can focus on your job and your family and and life and really get the joy and fulfilment you missed feeling earlier. You set yourself up to being prepared for that unknown future, because most folks sadly end up sleepwalking into their future and before they know it they are in their 60s or 70s and wonder how they got there with so little in savings and investments.

Yes it's boring making plans, boring making a strategy for yourself and even more boring to actually take active investing decision and actions…

This is because it seems like a lot of homework is required. But it will be worth it. Good planning and good governance will triumph over lazy, bad, ill thought financial fuzziness! There is a ton of useful information out there related to the FIRE community. You have to go out and seek it because no one will come to you with all the answers. *You have to do the work, no one can do this for you!*

Be and own the entire market…

As John Bogle used to say, the man who founded Vanguard, a truly excellent company that absolutely serves the normal average retail investors so well, if you own the entire market no one can accuse you of being biased because you are so well diversified in your investment philosophy and asset allocation policy. In other words for normal average retail investors it is better to be beta, better to be the market, because that's how you are guaranteed to build wealth in the long run in a simple and common sense way without incurring excess market risk, or paying excess fund management fees.

Passive index investors beat active funds in a matter of time…

Obviously people are not entirely alpha or beta, but most people believe they can beat the market (alpha behaviour) as well as the tens of thousands of active fund managers out there. Alpha behavioural decisions result in over-trading in a given active mutual fund. This just creates more cost and fees not to mention adding market risk for investors (compared to just sticking with passive index funds).

Did you know that in the long run, over a 10 or 20 year period, something like over 90% or up to 99% of index funds (e.g. S&P500) end up beating all actively managed mutual funds. So what are you paying for when you are hiring these expensive financial advisory firms pushing actively managed funds?! *Or is it financial derisory firms?!*

For fun go to Vegas…

Of course, I'm not saying don't gamble ever and if you still want a bit of excitement in your life you can always play with one or two percent of your total net worth into 'higher risk' strategies like stock picking or day trading or go play poker in Vegas! Or maybe want to buy some exotic digital commodities like crypto (which I do not understand so I keep well away).

Commodities are not investments, they are speculations…

Side note: So called commodities like digital currency are not an investment asset class because commodities pay no dividends or income or coupon rate.

And just like every other commodity, gold silver, pork bellies or frozen orange juice (think of the film Trading Places!) please remember that these are physical objects (or digital objects) meant for trading and speculating. These are not financial instruments meant for long term investors.

You can't fault The Intelligent Investor…

A true long term investor is only interested in investing in true financial instruments that produce a dividend, or coupon or income.

This is an important point, because as Professor Ben Graham, who wrote the book "The Intelligent Investor in 1949 said, **an investment is a financial instrument that produces a coupon or income, and everything else is a speculation!** _Please please please remember this fundamental take-away about investment vs speculation_. This is the one point in the entire book of 300 plus pages that resonated for me so strongly that it clarified for my simple brain 'what the hell is an investment' and 'what the hell is a pure trading/speculation activity'.

The unit price of a company share is a function of?…

So to be clear, an investment is something which produces an income so this could be a buy to let flat which is producing an income which you can measure over time. And the same is also true of company shares in mutual funds, because companies pay a dividend (income) over time to their shareholders (according to John Bogle in his Little Book of Common Sense

Investing, the share price performance over time of any listed company is partly determined by the firm's dividend policy and partly by the actions of traders buying and selling shares in that company – which also causes the share price to move up or down).

So the takeaway here is to be highly wary of things which are *not* buy to let flats and *not* low-cost index funds, where there is a promise that you will be earning extraordinary market returns. *If such schemes and scams are presented to you, please learn to spot them then run away in the opposite direction!*

Stick to these 2 asset classes (index funds and flats) and you will be happy…

IMO the only two asset classes you need to focus on are low-cost index funds and buy to let flats. These are the only kinds of asset classes that make the most sense for normal standard retail investors like us. You can forget everything else because they will probably turn out to be schemes or scams or high risk algorithmic trading or crypto(!) and definitely a guaranteed way of losing all or most of your money.

Don't think setting up a company is easy and you will win!…

Of course, if you are really bold you can also go ahead and set up a company because a successful company could also look after you for the rest of your life. Just remember though that 80% or more of small business start ups like restaurants fail in the first few years of opening! But, you are free to do what you want and as long as you're prepared to put in the hard work and take the knocks you may make it. But just like commodities, business is all about trading so you need to figure out what is your USP – unique selling point - otherwise the machinations of the market will smash your plan and decimate your wealth to pieces in 1 to 3 years.

Do you really think that the market cares about you?…

Remember that the market does not care about you. What's even worse is we as humans are utterly abysmal at reading risk or 'sizing the market'. We talk a big game thinking we've got the market conditions under control, then a disaster strikes and you are filing for bankruptcy. Ego gets you into trouble but no one will admit their ego is out of control. Just keep things simple and try to focus on being the best and operate in a sphere of excellence with humility that keeps you in the top 10-20% of your sector.

Over 80% of start ups fail…

To prove this point about ego, when one restaurant closes, another three may open up because they all want a) guaranteed success and b) open multiple outlets. IMO for a novice to set up a gym or a restaurant is completely delusional because most small start ups have an incredibly high failure rate in the first 3 years of opening, yet so many new small entrants in legacy businesses truly believe they can succeed where others failed. *This is delusional.*

Buffet hates gold...

Back to trading commodities. Even Warren Buffett doesn't like the commodity game like Gold because it is just a heavy lump of metal that produces no income...it just sits there in your safe or gets displayed as jewellery. Yes it has industrial uses, but apart from that it doesn't produce any income. So say you can buy $1 billion worth of gold and you'll have to store it somewhere and then hope it might be worth more in the future. Or, you could have $1 billion in cold hard cash and you could unleash this it into the global financial markets and buy ownership stakes in lots and lots of the worlds best companies. Now the $1 billion is working for you by producing dividends and growth.

Index funds allow everyone to own the world...

With index funds you literally become a part owner in all of the best companies on the planet. In our case it's over 10,000 globally listed companies in just a few index funds! **You develop a massive portfolio of companies with the end in mind being that you are generating some income (dividends) and growth (based on time in the market).** Remember also that smaller listed or really smaller non-listed companies get purchased by the best listed companies, so for you the average retail investor passive index investing is a win-win.

Be smart, be beta…

In summary, you have to decide what you are, alpha or beta. This means you have to know thyself and know your appetite for risk. Spoiler alert. If you have a massive ego and think you know best, things could end quite unwell for you (financially speaking and perhaps also in your chosen career). But, if we take a more measured and calm approach to investing in the markets and stick to a 'beta-mindset' and keep buying passive index funds, the long term performance ends up beating the vast majority of all actively managed funds when you consider a 10-20 year time horizon.

7. Stock market is the greatest wealth creating tool

Broadly yes. How else do you think (some of) the really rich get rich and live time free… they don't work like normal folks do, they live off their investments and are free to spend their time as they see fit. I am not saying all really rich people sit around and do nothing all day! No…what I mean is they do not depend on one main job for income or to pay bills… so that's the essence of what time-freedom means!

Tony Robbins in one interview for his book Unshakeable stated that thinking like the rich means you have to be an investor, because investors are asset owners

So rich people are natural investors because they keep buying income-earning assets.

Rich people buy investments but poor people buy things! (I think I once heard the Rich Dad, Poor Dad author make this point in a podcast). For the normal average retail investor who wants to ensure there is a runway of financial reserves leftover at the end of their working life, all they need to do is keep buying slices of real global companies listed all over the world via low-cost broad-based global index funds…bit by bit, month by month, year by year and let time in the global financial markets and compound interest do the rest. Just do what the rich do! Start early, drip feed money into the markets each month is the 'guaranteed' way for normal average retail investors to build financial wealth according to their income, savings rate and payment automation behaviours.

It's the amount of time your money spends in the markets (decades and decades) that leads to an accumulation of units and creation of value thanks to the power of compound interest. Otherwise (at least in the UK/US) the only default option is to wait until reaching nearly 70 years of age before collecting a modest state pension/social security. Getting access to your money sooner when you are healthy is better than waiting until old age when the desire to do things, to travel and to be adventurous wanes! *Don't wait until its too late to have fun! According to Warren Buffet in one interview he said that waiting until old age to have fun is a bad idea.*

8. What about property?

If it is a real flat or house in you name, then barring some fantastically unlucky form of ID theft, this is your asset and no one can steal it. Property is a form of wealth that is asset-backed in your name. If you need to monetise your property, you simply sell it. Sure it may take a month to six to sell it but fine, the property asset will convert into cash in time.

For example, you can consider a studio flat or a one bedroom or a two bedroom flat as easy to buy and easy to sell (fungible) assets. This means that they should be relatively easy to put back into the market and sell to a new buyer if you ever need to get your hands on liquid cash.

What you must avoid at all cost is any kind of fractional ownership, fractional investment scheme or unqualified collective investment scheme. These kind of investment schemes are not real investments as they are usually set up by individuals who form 'private wealth or property management' companies whom you have never heard of, whose partners you have never met, who have no real business history and could up up being fly by night operators or downright scams!

If you stand for nothing you will fall for anything and these schemes are designed to prize cash out of your bank accounts and into theirs! Just stay awake and steer clear of such shiny schemes and just stick with studio or one bedroom or two bedroom flats in any major city as long as the flat is in your name. Stick with a reliable agent who will find you a tenant and then you will start generating cash flow. It will take time, especially if you have a mortgage on these buy to let properties. No need to over do it, a few to five properties is fine then focus on index funds for additional wealth growth.

Whilst we are now debt free this was not the case as we were acquiring properties. In the beginning like most folks we had to leverage and borrow money in the form of a mortgage in order to afford our first and second (and so on) buy to let flats, and as we continued that process, later we were able to just purchase flats with cash without the need for any mortgage. This means you immediately start generating positive cash flow. Remember you just stick to these kinds of properties, and of course low cost index funds, and ignore all other asset classes because we are normal average retail investors.

9. Mutual funds are essential for your wealth to grow –but come in two styles, Active (alpha) vs. Passive (beta)

There is a ton of literature out there about the distinctive difference between active mutual funds and passive index funds. I would advise that you do your own research on this, but then try to understand the monetary impact that fees can have on your total fund performance over at 10 to 30 year period. When you have total annual expense ratios of over 1% or over 2% of your total fund value, paid to your advisor as fees, the impact of such fees is to eat one third to two thirds of the funds total future performance. This means the poor old investor ends up with very little net return. Meanwhile your advisor is driving around in a fancy car paid for by you!

That is why it is imperative to keep your total investment fund management expense ratios to below 1%. You only have to look on Vanguard's website and check in on a few funds to see how low they charge. There are funds like S&P 500 where you're paying less than 10 basis points (that is less than 0.1%) and some other funds, maybe a global fund - which could be 15 to 20 basis points. This is critical to winning in the long run if you can manage to guarantee to pay ultra low and efficient investment fund fees.

10.   Track income and wealth - measure and monitor

Before reaching FI I started tracking our income and expenses and assets and liabilities way back in January 2015! I made my own spreadsheet in excel then became quite obsessed with it. I kept tweaking it and improving and developing it, and I still use it from time to time today. It is an absolutely mammoth excel workbook now, but each tab is very clearly explicable in terms of assets, liabilities, income, expenses, renting vs buying a car and over a decade's worth of buy to let tax statements of income, expenses and net profit after tax.

I also managed to work out - over a 15 year period of living in the UAE and owning a total of five vehicles in this period - what is the true cost of car ownership in fils or pence per kilometre. Boring! Who does this? I do because I tracked every component of spending, and even with cars I tracked the cost of depreciation, the cost of annual insurance and registration and annual maintenance and of course fuel. I would enter all weekly expenses into the excel during weekends.

As I said earlier, unless you measure it, how can you possibly monitor something? And I truly believe that YOU having your own cool wealth spreadsheet which tracks everything (a bit like you are running a small business) will be a critical success factor in your own financial journeys. As the years go by, you will see your wealth grow. Without a cool spreadsheet, everything you say (or think) about what you think your net worth is, is a guess or puffery!

My excel even has a tab which works out cash flows 20 years into the future! Yes I know that's a hell of a stretch but actually it's important now that we've stepped off the work train, to see how well things can continue the way they are, and then also see the effect of future extra income such as state pensions coming in within the next 10 years. So you should be able to account for all of the different sort of income streams coming into your household, and then also all of the different sort of costs that are steady state or lumpy like uni fees.

If you measure everything correctly e.g. on a monthly basis, you can figure out your net worth down to the last dollar or pound. I did, but then I was a bit obsessive about the whole process (because early in my career, I was one of those excel modelling experts hired by professional consulting firms to build telecom network cost models for clients all over the world).

Excel is easy to use and you don't need a big brain to use it for your personal finance matters. Keep the excel tracker simple so that it's easy to spot errors, fix mistakes and keep refining and fine-tuning it.

I would say you should trust this meticulous process of budgeting and tracking your financial activity (income and spend) and count everything.

Otherwise with no comprehension of your financial situation now and where you want to be is just like wishing and hoping and driving blind. I mean I had a life, but I also lived in my spreadsheet week to month to quarter and year. I would monitor everything - assets, liabilities, income and spend, make projections, try to also track our lifetime income. Probably a bit obsessive, but it worked for me/it worked for us as a family.

I once came across an interesting metric called 'LWI' which is a bit crude but quite interesting. So apart from just understanding the meaning of net worth, LWI stands for Lifetime Wealth-to-Income. It's a ratio of total net worth divided by all your lifetime income. Broadly speaking, the older we get, the higher the LWI ratio becomes but when you start work in your 20s, the ratio is understandably pretty low. But then if you keep acquiring investable assets in your 20s and 30s right the way through to your 40s and 50s, the ratio remarkably ends up being quite close to 1!

LWI = Lifetime Wealth / Lifetime Income* (* item to measure income as net income after taxes and fees, as otherwise gross income would be a bit misleading in my view).

11. Remind yourself of the super resources of life.

In the past, I would sometimes ask people, so what do you think of the super resources of life? They would say things likes water and food or money. I will try to challenge them by thinking in terms of time and how time is a depleting and non-renewable resource and so if you were able to stop working in your 40s or 50s instead of your 60s or 70s you end up creating an 'extra' time buffer of 20 years where you decide you can do what you want.

It was in 2017 that I became involved with the FIRE group in Dubai called Simply FI that also led to a number of talks by Andrew Hallam (Millionaire Teacher). From all those talks and a few side discussions with the organisers I got a strong sense that FIRE is worth pursuing because when you achieve 'enough' you also get to have you time back – which is definitely one of the great life hacks.

Apart from the time, the other super resources of life are probably health and ability to continuously learn. So it absolutely makes sense to operate with a healthy mind and a healthy body. Because everybody knows folks who have serious health dispositions end up being trapped in their own bodies …

bringing an end to freedom of choice to do lots of things such as travelling, driving, shopping and going out for walks.

12.   Watch out for opportunities - be mindful and alert of all the noises.

Broadly speaking, most average retail investors are ordinary people who are not sophisticated when it comes to financial markets (that's you and I). So in that case they only need to focus on the simplicity of two investment asset classes. The first one is the financial markets or the stock markets where you are trying to accumulate wealth by buying low cost index funds every month - set it and forget it. The second one is classic buy to let properties e.g. one or two bedroom flats in any major city or town in a country market you are familiar with and know how it operates because a) property is a very personal kind of asset allocation and b) you want to generate a healthy flow of passive income.

If you literally just stick to low cost index funds and buy to let flats you probably do not need to do anything else (apart from maxing out any company pension schemes you have).

Then you can avoid reading financial papers or watching the financial news, and also ignore invitations to invest in different kinds of schemes from cold callers. Never ever get seduced by glossy marketing brochures or media campaigns about different kinds of 'investment schemes' in different countries like timeshare, student pods, care home and hotel rooms.

Remember these kind of schemes mean you have zero control over them. You're handing your money over to some private entity, to people whom you have never met nor do you know their business history, yet it is they who decide what happens to your money. Can you really trust any schemes that makes promises of guaranteed returns? No. You can't.

Whereas if you simply focus on flats and/or index funds, these are investments which are tried and tested and they are in your name and you have full 100% ownership and control over these investments. With flats you can either manage them yourself or, as we do, use letting agents which is fine. It's a cliché, but I use agents and accountants because I prefer to work 'on the business' and not 'in the business'.

With mutual funds you can, of course use a financial advisor, but remember it's so easy for any average retail investor to set up an account (e.g. with Vanguard) in your name and choose amongst a few broad-based index funds, invest every month and automate these investments, so you pay yourself first, meaning you invest first out of the income that you make, and then you can spend the rest for yourself.

It's not complicated, its simple. But the financial advisory industry is paid to make it seem complicated and difficult for the normal average retail investor to 'take control' of their finances.

13.   Risk - you will not see it coming because you can't gauge it

Over the past two decades I've had so many interviews with different financial advisors who perform some sort of rudimentary interview to try to gauge your appetite for risk. This is a completely arbitrary and useless test because most average retail investors cannot define risk let alone assess it. They have no idea what it means in the context of the stock market let alone generally to the usual standard range of life altering decisions.

Putting this slightly differently, in a company environment a corporation makes decisions on a risk-adjusted basis. All large corporate entities (like all companies in global index funds!) have incredibly smart and widespread professional teams whose job is to assess, manage and mitigate risk on behalf of the entire company, and by implication the shareholders - the ultimate owners of all publicly listed companies in the world.

When it comes to us regular folks, we tend to rush big decisions. We tend not to take a measured approach and we certainly do not know how to do risk assessment. So this is where you have to figure out your own understanding of what market risk means versus what a crazy level of risk means versus complete and outright scams. *Sadly people who think the stock market is a* _gamble like going to Vegas are highly uninformed (this is the 'before FIRE' phase)._

There are lots and lots of highly risky questionable 'investment schemes' that claim to offer unbelievable returns (compared to the market returns or beta) and some that even promise you a "guaranteed" return for x number of years. No one can guarantee future returns, but nothing stops schemers making such bold claims about their schemes to attract your attention. Treat this as a massive red flag or an indicator of how faulty such schemes are and designed simply to grab your attention and take you money!

14. Risk - scammers and schemers will lead to failed investments if you are led astray.

Just remember to never to get seduced by a cold call invitation as they are designed to take your money in return for an ownership scheme in, for example, a student room, care home room or a hotel room, or a holiday timeshare or a solar park or some form of green energy scheme, or biodiversity farming scheme, etc. Be warned - don't do it. Speak to anyone in your network who is more enlightened about the investment landscape about such schemes, but do not make any kind of decision on any kind of wacky exotic investment scheme on your own.

Believe me when a fool rushes in he/you will live to regret it. Remember there is the thing called survivorship bias, which roughly speaking, describes people who just talk about their successes when in reality, most people have made financial errors, but will never ever discuss them because errors are embarrassing. Hence never go it alone and find a smarter person in your network to have an open discussion, figure out if the idea is sound. Never make a big financial decision in isolation. Or just keep it simple (index funds and property).

15. Stillness –control, don't over react, else ego will crush you

Be careful not to rush into financial decision-making just because of something you read in the press, or see in the news media. Definitely don't listen to the guy in the coffee shop. What you find is that everybody has their investment preference or bias. Some people like property as a means to building a 'pension-pot' for passive income and others like the stock market, or just buying bonds or only saving cash in a building society account. You don't want to be too one-sided in these matters.

The less diversified you are, the more financial market risk you take on and the greater your opportunity cost of earning a global market benchmark level of return. *(now this may sound counter-intuitive) The greater your asset allocation decisions are more and more diversified to the point of owning thousands and thousands of the worlds biggest and best listed companies, the more likely your returns will align with global stock market benchmark returns. You want to 'be the market' so that you are fully diversified, otherwise the opposite is that your focus is too narrow, or too one sided, and this is where you miss out on returns year-in and year-out (leaving money on the table!).*

When it comes to managing your financial money matters the bigger your ego, the bigger the fall. So try to be wise and centred. Keep your investment policy simple and consistent, make more correct decisions and way less bad decisions. And if you just stick to real investment asset classes like index funds and rental property income, you can ignore all the rest of the schemes that are out there, including commodities like gold or even faux commodities, like crypto and all sorts of other types of collective investment schemes, or fractional ownership schemes. Just ignore them and you should be fine. *Don't worry about FOMO (Fear of Missing Out).*

Or as Warren Buffett says, just stick to things you understand and avoid everything that you don't understand, will work out to be better for you. Because usually the news, media and ADVISORS and cold callers all have a communication strategy that work on your 'fear and greed' brain receptors. *Just get to know the patter and you'll be able to see it a mile off.*

16.   Strategy, Planning & Initiatives (offence and defence)

At the end of the day, you've got to have a plan. And with a plan comes having a strategy and figuring out your particular initiatives to make sure your financial strategy comes into play. This is a slow burn game that takes one to two decades to create your own freedom fighting fund that let's you have options later on for your ideal work/life balance.

It's not something you can rush because for the vast majority of all of us getting rich or wealthy 'enough' takes time. And on that note we can create constructs based on sport to see how we can improve our offence and defence. Offence means how to maintain and grow income over time and defence means how we are managing and controlling our spend, savings and sound investing behaviour.

Having no plan means you just drift without a solid sense of purpose or direction and you are just about managing the status quo of your life, or are happy to let one decade slip into the next without paying any attention to your personal finance situation.

You can still make the right moves but also be ignorant about why you made those moves! Up to the age of 51, we did do one thing right, which was to acquire some properties which are investable assets which produce an income. But this was too one-sided because of a complete lack of FIRE knowledge and know how. In that sense I was ignorant about the possibilities of acquiring other asset classes as another way of building wealth - such as broad-based index funds, because I was too afraid to invest in the stock markets by myself. Not anymore and not since 2017 which is all thanks to the FIRE community!

So the lesson is you don't want to be too one-sided, and you want to try and be as diversified as possible. When you own a stake in over 10,000 of the best companies in the world, this is called being truly globally diversified. Furthermore, in terms of being on the offence, this is also where you take a position about how much debt you have and how aggressive you want to be in terms of over paying that debt because this also has an effect on your net income from all your property investments.

As I write this, there's a lot of folks out there hurting because of the significant recent increases in interest rates broadly 13-14 years after the Global Financial Crisis of 2008/9. I took the decision in 2017 that apart from building index funds I would also try to figure out an optimal 'debt-reduction' plan in order to grow our passive property income so that it supported our lifestyle. This meant dealing with the mortgage debt head on, putting a plan into place to pay it all off in 3-5 years and also building a healthy emergency fund. So planning can take on a lot of different objectives as long as you can design it and govern it in a very cool excel spreadsheet (which I did).

I have a chart somewhere in my wealth workbook which shows just how dramatic the impact of debt-reduction can be over a 10 year period, and how the debt reduction absolutely correlates with wealth accumulation over time. And not only that, I superimposed a line for a decade's worth of net income from the property investments. As I expected, the debt level decline correlated with net wealth growth, as well as net income growth. It's a beautiful chart!

There's so many debates about mortgages, should I pay it off or keep it and invest the extra cash into the markets? At the end of the day, paying off debt is not a bad idea and thankfully I planned it when interest rates were at minuscule base rate levels compared to what's happened in the last 2-3 years. It's a personal decision because its personal finance and if it feels right for you to pay down debt, then it's a correct decision for you.

17. Keep learning – so many resources, podcasts and commentators who want to help you.

As Stephen Covey of Seven Habits fame, quite rightly suggests, you must keep sharpening your tools, so it is important to keep yourself urbane and up to date with information, but also feel confident that you are using the right kind of professionals to support your journey. This is the way you understand what the correct process for tax (by employing a great accountant) is or undertaking a property transaction (by using an experienced agent). Based on personal experience I promise you that you will tire of people in your network telling you 'you should do this' or 'you should do that' or 'this is the tax that applies' or 'this is how you can pay nothing for property agency fees' when you soon realise that they're talking nonsense and it is better to consult and use real professionals in this regard.

Generally speaking your pub and coffee shop mates are not going to make you rich or change your financial destiny! Only you can make you rich by having a simple and consistent investment policy and sticking to it (so you are not distracted by charlatan peeps and schemes).

By all means listen to the ideas of others but don't fall for anything that is beyond your comprehension or outside the scope of your investment policy such as simple tried and tested investment asset classes. Let them have their say and don't react. Stick to your winning plan since this is the right plan for you. IMO everything outside index funds and properties is noise.

Clearly we're not saving the world here, but we *are* saving ourselves from ourselves since we can be our own worst enemy when it comes of making financial investment decisions. Index funds (and/or properties) are simple and all we are doing is optimising our lives using the power of personal finance to hopefully enhance our lives, happiness and wellbeing.

18.   Inflation is damaging –be aware, so because of it you have to be an asset owner.

Sure, you can make lots of money and just take it in the bank and earn zero to very little interest on that. This is certainly the approach of our parent's generation who as immigrants to the UK would work extremely hard for very low wages.

Yet despite this they still managed to achieve a decent savings rate but just put all their money into building societies or banks for a rainy day. The problem is that money ends up becoming eroded over time thanks to the power of inflation. So in my view, the best hedges against inflation boils down to 2 widely popular and easy to understand asset classes, index funds, and property, that's it.

Stick to these two asset classes and you'll be fine over time. Don't worry about the ups and downs of the market and don't get all reactive and upset. Just enjoy the ride. That's what investors do, they buy and hold and stay quiet.

What you can do is keep a small part your total wealth as cash such as a few percent to five or ten. It's your call . Just remember that inflation erodes the value of cash and so when you reach that point where you have a little bit of excess cash left over that is above what you need in an emergency fund, put that excess cash to work! When the money works for you, it works for you 24/7, 365 days a year. If it sits in your bank account, this is a lost opportunity. Remember money never sleeps. It never get sick. It does not discriminate (meaning it does not care who owns it). It just keeps working 24/7…great!

19.   In the pyramid scheme of life, aim for the top 20%.

At the end of the day in the pyramid scheme of life, it seems pretty good at the top and it seems pretty hard and competitive at the bottom. You need to figure out your skillset and how to place them in in the market sector where do you want to position yourself in the pyramid of life. I would also say try to aim your career ambition to being in the top 10-20% of your peer group because promotions and shifting between companies are a useful way to create more income growth.

When you come from a modest upbringing, it's actually hard to make big spending decisions, even though you know you can afford it. We could eat out in restaurants every night of the week, but then this could become quite sickly and tiresome.

We could go on lots of lavish holidays which could also be excessive and tiring. What's interesting though is that money can allow you to hop around and live between two or even three locations in the world. This is a less tiring way to live in different countries because it's a slow burn existence where you can live like a local!

As I write this, we now live between UK and UAE, and I never thought I would ever reach a point to be able to operate this kind of lifestyle. It's a fun existence with a sense of freedom and adventure but without being too tiring (which by definition 'fast travel' and 'short hops' and 'annual leave' days from work can make you feel quite burned because such travel involves rushing around during peak holiday periods).

20. Too much debt means more years of work...

A mortgage on a property could be regarded as a good debt because you're buying an asset which potentially could appreciate over time. On the other hand being addicted to a consumerist lifestyle bankrolled by credit cards could end up crippling you. I prefer to be on the side of compound interest where over time in the stock markets your money and wealth accumulates. But at the same time, I prefer not to work for debt interest namely credit card and mortgage debt! So this is up to you to decide which side of compound interest do you prefer to be on.

Of course, the trouble with financing is that maybe you want to give a certain impression of a lifestyle to others (The Joneses). Really what's the point in that? You're trying to show off to people you don't even know and at the end of the day you become a debt slave working all the hours to meet the interest payments. The bigger the debt the more years of working for the man are required. Remember, counting the time it takes to commute to work and back, a typical professional job probably requires 1,800 to 2,000 total hours of time commitment a year!

This is how the system is set up to keep you on the spending train and work train forever! For more than is necessary, I don't think that's the right answer to be stuck in an office all day or stuck in a car/train for an hour or two a day! It's better to be in control of your destiny. We work, work and work, yet it is scary that maybe up to half of all households in the western world would probably struggle to find $100 to $1000 to cover an emergency! This is literally a paycheque to paycheque existence. You will feel much more resilient and comfortable if you can build a financial buffer around you and withstand and handle any kind of financial knock, shock or emergency.

21.   Teach your kids pass it on so they are prepared for life.

Pretty much, most folks, never ever ever talk about money, financial matters and investing as it relates to the ordinary common retail person. The same is true for households, and probably most parents don't discuss these type of matters with the kids because they never discuss it amongst themselves! I believe such discussions are a worthwhile endeavour that reap out-sized returns later in life. How else are you going to set your kids up to understand what is the point of money and how to operate with it and how to live and how to budget and so on.

Such discussions with the next generation are healthy and holistic and will have a tremendous impact on your children's lives and that is why I put these notes together. But I've also had the fortunate ability and patience to drip-feed to our sons bits and pieces of financial education topics in conversation without making it complicated.

The thing is, it's not that complicated and any average brain can take control of their financial destiny with planning, intention and action! Your wheel of fortune requires many steps: finish education and training, start work with the first job, earn income start saving, set aside emergency funds, invest the gap between income and spend – automatically into broad based low cost index funds on a monthly (set it and forget it!). Then with patience and decades in the markets plus the power of compound interest - the wheel of fortune delivers.

22.   Financial intelligence checklist...

Below is just a short checklist of thoughts, ideas and take-aways to be mindful of Financial Education / Financial Intelligence 'fintel' is not taught in schools.

This is your chance to close the gap by learning, by taking an active interest in your personal finance journey (which requires planning, active decision making and setting up expectations of what you want to achieve and when you want to step off the work-treadmill).

There is no intellectual property on many great thoughts and ideas about money, finance and investing. Be wiser - read, learn, discuss with likeminded folks, exchange common sense saving and investment ideas. There is no better place to start than with the FIRE Community.

Greatest gifts in life are your mind and your time and your talent to convert all of this into money. But requires self-awareness, humility, willingness to learn (you must lose ego - when it comes to investing – because we are our own worst enemy)

Talking means sharing. Find someone who is genuinely interested in helping you, with no vested interest. Your intuition will tell you if this is a genuine person or someone with a hidden agenda.

FIRE knowledge and know how. Use 100+ hours to learn about saving and investing. In a life of 30,000 days this is not much sacrifice to help fill any basic common sense knowledge gaps.

Build a sound financial foundation, to support a skyscraper! If you don't, it could come tumbling down.

Our duty is to spend and invest time and money as wisely as possible. You will build wealth with patience and knowledge and remember there is no truth in the notion often touted in the social media about getting rich quick.

Knowing who you are is a good starting point. Do you want to be an owner, an investor, or are you thinking, behaving and acting like a high risk alpha trader, a speculator. The latter leads to cash/wealth loss, meaning you could lose your entire stake. The former is aligned to long term value investing approach – like Professor Benjamin Graham advocated in The Intelligent Investor (1949) and who taught Warren Buffet, his student, who simply applied the principles of value-investing.

Warren Buffet is about 'buy and hold' investable assets, and about how for the average retail investor it is probably best to just buy low-cost index tracker funds. Do this over a long time, being patient and disciplined about money, paying yourself first (saving consistently on a monthly basis), means you will more likely get to the end goal of building a sustainable freedom fund for yourself to drawdown on when you want to, or need to stop working.

Keynes in his 'General Theory' said 'the future is unknowable'. So it is best NOT to make uninformed risky decisions vs. Aiming to make more manageable risk-controlled/managed financial decisions. Do not listen to mates in the pub or your mates in the City or talking heads on the financial news channels. Their job is to sound flash, confuse you and complicate your mind so you take the hit, buy their stock picks or actively managed funds and they take high annual fees to 'manage your money'.

Finally, do not trust anyone and agree that only YOU have your best interests at heart. No one cares about you apart from you and you are not in other people's future plans. Your financial journey is yours and yours to start, manage, govern, oversee, tweak and optimise for the rest of your life.

The is no benevolent dictator behind the scenes making sure you will be okay in your financial future. This absolutely means YOU cannot avoid financial intelligence learning because otherwise without YOUR active decision making in financial investment matters, you will be working on life's other matters in an active way, but passively accept your financial destiny based not on your actions but the actions and decisions of others underwritten by your sub-optimal level of fintel.

Remember, there is no magic potion to growing money. All fintel, requires some basic knowledge, patience, time and your respect for it because of what money can do for you. Money is just a tool, an enabler that hopefully a) creates for you a brighter financial future and b) more work/life balance options.

23.   Financial Freedom is a process –and one of the greatest life hacks!

As I reflect on 32 years of working, of course, in the beginning it was all great fun building a career, as you move from company to company and you are learning and working with great talented people and bosses and you are trying your best to add value and see the rewards come in. This is true for everybody but as you get older things will change. Either you change, or your company changes, or the external environment in which your company operates changes. These are the vagaries of life!

These change-agents may cause you to reconsider if you are still in the right job or if you want to continue doing the job that you're doing because obviously at times high power jobs can also be quite stressful. This is life in the fast lane of high skill fluid-intelligent jobs as Professor Jordan Peterson stated in one of his lectures. So yes you are being rewarded well, but you also have to manage the stress and responsibility of keeping and maintaining your position to a high standard.

FI creates an option path for you to choose when to walk away for good or take a break or downsize your commitments from full time to part time. FI is a great life hack because having financial resources enables you to plan,

execute and then allow you to enjoy your time and move on to other
endeavours on your terms before real old age sets in.

24. So what's your plan? When to start? Keep it simple.

So they say the best time to start was yesterday, and if not yesterday then today, and if not today then tomorrow! The sooner you start the better and that's why when someone has completed their education in their early 20s they could potentially shave 10-20 years from the default option of 40-50 years of full time working by planning now to create their own financial freedom fund. Having 'enough' wealth and knowing what enough means will give you all the options you need to optimise your work/life balance.

I truly wish you good luck in all your future financial planning and decision making.